CW01498002

Dog Aggression Management

The Comprehensive Training Guide Managing Behavior & Aggressive Prevention in Dogs

Hazel W. Wright

Dog Aggressions Management

Dog Aggressions Management

techniques outlined in this book.

By reading this document, the reader agrees that under no circumstances is the author responsible for any losses, direct or indirect, that are incurred as a result of the use of the information contained within this document, including, but not limited to, errors, omissions, or inaccuracies.

Bluesource And Friends

This book is brought to you by Bluesource And Friends, a happy book publishing company.

Our motto is **"Happiness Within Pages"**

We promise to deliver amazing value to readers with our books.

We also appreciate honest book reviews from our readers.

Connect with us on our Facebook page www.facebook.com/bluesourceandfriends and stay tuned to our latest book promotions and free giveaways.

Don't forget to claim your FREE books!

Brain Teasers:

https://tinyurl.com/karenbrainteasers

Harry Potter Trivia:
https://tinyurl.com/wizardworldtrivia
Sherlock Puzzle Book (Volume 2)

https://tinyurl.com/Sherlockpuzzlebook2

Also check out our other books

"67 Lateral Thinking Puzzles"

https://tinyurl.com/thinkingandriddles

"Rookstorm Online Saga"

https://tinyurl.com/rookstorm

"Korman's Prayer"

https://tinyurl.com/kormanprayer

"The Convergence"

https://tinyurl.com/bloodcavefiction

"The Hardest Sudokos In Existence (Ranked As The Hardest Sudoku Collection Available In The Western World)"

https://tinyurl.com/MasakiSudoku

Dog Aggressions Management

Table of Contents

Dog Aggressions Management

Dog Aggressions Management

Dog Aggressions Management

Introduction

In the current day and age, we are lucky to have as much knowledge as we do about dogs and the way they tick. Going back 20 or 30 years, the techniques for dealing with dog aggression were *highly questionable*. I remember taking my beloved Spot to a dog trainer a good few years ago. Spot, a rescued Collie mix, had been struggling with possessive aggression regarding his food and toys. He was an incredibly sweet and timid dog, but he would occasionally growl or snap if you tried to take away his empty bowl or pick up one of his toys.

This trainer that I took him to was supposed to be a bit of a miracle worker, but I was far from impressed once I arrived. I vividly remember those first moments between my beloved pet and the trainer. Spot was grabbed by the back of the neck and forced into a choke chain and muzzle without the trainer even evaluating the dog in front of him. It seemed to be standard procedure for every animal that came through their doors.

Now, I can't fault people for being careful; that is perfectly understandable, but as we will cover in this book, it is better to treat an aggressive dog like a scared child than like Hannibal Lecter.

This trainer then proceeded to demonstrate a "trick" he promised would solve *any* issues with *any* dog. This method was known as the "alpha roll" (flipping a dog onto their back and pinning them down until they stop fighting back) and it did nothing but terrify my poor companion. This method may be effective at curbing dog aggression, but that's only through scaring the living daylights out of our pets.

See, the alpha roll is a move designed to show total dominance. In dog language, it's the equivalent of holding a knife to someone's throat. For most animals, the stomach is their most vulnerable point, and this is the area of their body they naturally try to protect at all times. This is why your friendly childhood dog may even push your hand away or gently mouth it while you pat its tummy.

I'm not sure if the trainer was just ignorant of dog psychology or if they were just completely uncaring about the animal's well-being. But, seeing the fear on my pet's face and his cowering afterward made me determined to find a better way to help him. The alpha roll was a no-go for me; instead, I began investigating other methods.

Dog Aggressions Management

During my subsequent investigations, I ended up gaining the necessary knowledge to become a qualified dog trainer myself with countless success stories under my belt. This may sound like a massive brag, but I know how it feels to put your pet in the hands of someone who doesn't seem to know what they're doing, and I wouldn't wish that on anyone!

At least three-quarters of the clients I see need help understanding and correcting their dog's aggressive behavior. The majority of these cases are very mild and involve easily correctable behavior. As long as their human is committed and willing to make the necessary environmental changes and assist behavioral development, 99 percent of cases can be a success story of their own. Every dog deserves to live a happy life, without having to resort to aggression to deal with its fears and anxieties.

What do I mean by **environmental changes** and **behavioral development**, you may ask?

Well, they may sound like relatively self-explanatory terms, but I assure you there is more to them than meets the eye.

Environmental changes refer to evaluating the environment your pet is in, finding out what causes their aggression, and removing the opportunity for aggressive behavior to happen. If your garden service mowing the lawn always causes an episode of aggression, make sure your territorial-aggressive dog is safely put in a room with the windows closed and his favorite chew toys to keep him occupied and distracted.

Behavioral development takes a bit more into account. To consider this, we need to take our dog's emotions and reactions to external stimuli that cause aggressive episodes and work on changing the way they view and respond to these stimuli. This means changing the way our dog perceives a threat by convincing them that whatever scares them isn't actually bad. Maybe your dog is aggressive towards the garbage collectors, and whenever he hears or sees them, he just barks and barks. One way we could fix this issue is to teach your dog that whenever the garbage collectors arrive, Fido gets a treat. If you know when the garbage truck is coming, you can prepare a small piece of chicken or ham and give your pet a treat at the first sign of barking. This may seem like we are rewarding their behavior, but provided we have diagnosed the correct source of their fear, we are actually teaching them that "garbage truck means a treat, so the garbage truck isn't bad."

Another method of behavioral development is giving

our pet a substitute behavior that replaces the aggressive behavior they relied on before. A dog that runs to the door and barks when they hear a car horn can be taught that a car horn is actually his signal to go and happily get a treat or toy from their human.

Overall, there are a few things I like to make sure every person who wants to help their pets knows:

- **Never rush it.** We're always told to let children learn at their own pace; well, the same holds true for dogs. Some dogs will learn faster than others, some are more stubborn, some are more cooperative. Behavioral development can take time; it's certainly not a process we want to rush our pet into. If anything, taking things too fast is just going to make the situation worse and scare your pet more.
- **There is never a quick fix.** Regardless of what you may hear from some trainers or read online, there is no magic spray bottle or special technique that will instantly help your dog behave better. It will take lots of time and effort, but if you invest that time, you will see lasting results.
- **Environmental changes should always come first.** You can never hope to make the

behavioral changes you want to achieve if there are still environmental triggers that may set off your pet. The very first thing we need to do is create a sterile and trigger-free environment for our pets. You should ensure your dog has an environment that never gives them the need or want to be aggressive.

- **Don't expect constant improvements.** You and your pet will have good days and bad days. Expect to make progress some days and have setbacks others. Consistency and perseverance are the only ways to ensure a positive long-term result.

The goal of this book is to help anyone with an aggressive dog have a better understanding of what canine aggression is, what causes it, and how we can help correct it with force-free methods that offer long-term results.

This book is written for pet owners who want to learn more and help bolster their ability to correct negative behavior in their pets. This is in no way a replacement for the services and help that a trained professional animal psychologist or trainer can provide. If your animal has frequent bouts of serious aggression, a history of dangerous behavior, or if you are afraid of your dog, please seek the help of a trained and qualified professional.

Part 1: Types of Aggression in Dogs

Chapter 1: Canine Social Systems and Aggression

Canine social systems and the various quirks they entail is a crucial subject to become familiar with if you hope to help your pet correct their unwanted behavior. Canine social structures can both be dizzyingly complex and incredibly simple. For those with no understanding of dog social behavior outside of the outdated and incorrect "alpha males and dominance" theory, this chapter may come as a shock to you.

Dogs have a totally different social system than wild animals, which means the article you may have read about wolves holds no weight here. Your dog and all the dogs they meet at the dog park have an ever-changing position in a social hierarchy that is all based on how they feel each day.

Understanding Social Systems

Dog Aggressions Management

Unlike wolves, the social structures of dogs are incredibly flexible and can change at any moment. See, with wolves, there is always a hierarchy that only ever changes if a stronger challenger comes along and overpowers those above them. There's always this talk of "alpha dogs" in every pack. The alphas lead, the betas are submissive to the alphas, and the omegas are submissive to the alphas and betas. It goes alpha, then beta, and lastly omega in the hierarchy. While this hierarchy is present in groups of dogs, it is very flexible and subject to change based on a lot of different factors.

The social standing of your dog depends completely on their confidence. This is what makes dog social structures so flexible. It all depends on the confidence of the dogs involved. Dog confidence levels are always changing depending on the day, how they feel, what environment they are in, and who is with them. Dogs that are naturally confident in all scenarios are actually very rare; they make up around four percent of the population. The vast majority of a dog's confidence will grow stronger or waver depending on what scenario they are in and how they choose to project themselves.

Canine Communication

When our dogs meet humans, other dogs, or other animals, they have three ways in which they will choose to communicate these are body language, verbal cues, and odors.

In comparison to the average dog, humans are body language illiterate and scent-blind. That makes it difficult for dogs to naturally communicate with us. Dogs adapt though, and soon enough, even the youngest of puppies will start to pick up human forms of communication. This often leads to dogs meeting us halfway and adapting their forms of communication to us. It's been noted by animal behaviorists that dogs use far more vocal cues (barks, whines, cries) when talking to humans than when communicating with other dogs or animals. This is because humans are naturally very good at making sense of sounds. We know that a snarl means "back off," a yelp means "help," and a happy bark means "let's play!" Of course, there are some more subtle cues we don't understand without some experience and learning, but we *can* learn.

Dogs have more emotions and thoughts than they can convey through just vocal cues though. So, to be good owners, we need to try and learn to better understand their methods of communication.

Body language is something we will cover, in part, later in the book with calming signals, but calming signals aren't the only facet of canine body language. Ask any expert in human body language and they will tell you that you can tell nearly everything about someone's personality just from your initial encounters with them and the subtle body language cues they give off. It's the same for dogs.

Dominance and Submission

Dogs rely completely on their body language to make first impressions when meeting other dogs. For example, let's say your dog meets another new dog at the park. While your dog walks up to them head-up, chest out, tail wagging happily, the other dog's tail is wagging a bit lower, its head is doing a nodding motion, and it's avoiding eye contact with your dog. In this situation, your dog is showing the more dominant body language and has put itself above the other dog in the hierarchy between the two.

Dog Aggressions Management

Keep in mind though, this is flexible. Maybe the next time these two dogs meet your dog is feeling under the weather, or the other dog has its owner nearby, or the environment has changed and your dog isn't as comfortable as before. These things and more could cause your dog to feel less confident, which might make them submissive to the other dog this time around. Most of the time, for dogs with normally developed social skills, this switch of hierarchy goes without any kind of bad feelings.

Dominant and submissive body language in dogs is all about the way your pet carries themself in their initial encounter with another dog. Some common examples of dominant body language may be a stiff and upright wagging tail, raised fur, a forward-facing posture, and direct eye contact. Submissive body language, on the other hand, is often shown through cues such as walking or crawling low to the ground, curling up to appear small and non-threatening, tucking tails between legs, and lots of licking.

Dogs Playing

Happy and Sad Body Communication

You may think because your dog is wagging its tail, that means it is happy. Well, that's not strictly true. Dogs have happy wags, sad wags, nervous wags, and just about every other emotion too. The same can be said for barks, facial expressions, and other forms of body language or communication. Understanding these finer details of your dog's communication can help you connect with your pets better and avoid any misunderstandings or unwanted situations in the future.

If your dog is happy, some very obvious cues will stand out to you, as well as some more subtle ones. While fast wagging tails are an obvious sign of happiness, a lot of people don't know that relaxed ears and neutral facial features are a sign of happiness too. Another sign of happiness we may see is the "downward dog" stretch. Often when you get up in the morning, return home from work, or see your pet for the first time in a few hours, you may notice them doing this stretch towards you. This gesture is actually a greeting of sorts; it shows submission but in a relaxed and friendly way.

Dog Aggressions Management

A happy dog will also frequently engage with you. If your dog is bringing you things, asking to be stroked, sitting with you, or in any way interacting with you or the things around you, chances are it is happy. If your dog wasn't completely comfortable and at home, they wouldn't be actively interacting and exploring the environment around them.

When it comes to sadness, it's easy to overlook changes of behavior in your dog that don't impact you. If your dog is aggressive, you notice it because it could hurt you or someone else. If your dog is playful, you notice it because they pester you to play. But, if your dog is sad, they will often just keep to themselves; this makes it hard for some of us to notice.

Dogs don't suffer from depression or sadness in the same way humans do. We don't know a lot about how they experience sadness. Some behaviors and cues can point towards whether your dog is sad though. For example, if your dog usually greets you with a fast wagging tail after work but suddenly stops, and that prolongs, there could be something that is making your dog feel concerned or unwell. A limp, non-wagging tail is one of the most prominent signs of unhappiness.

The ears of a dog are also incredibly expressive in this regard. When your pet is sad or concerned, its ears may be drawn flat on its head, and not in the relaxed pose they would be in if your dog is happy and not in the alert upright pose. Dogs also tend to isolate themselves when they are sad or unwell. If your dog is distancing themselves from you and others, like laying in an empty room, hiding under plants in the garden, or even sleeping away from everyone else, this may be a sign of unhappiness. Keep in mind, sadness in dogs is always either caused by anxiety in their environment or illness, so always get your dog checked by a vet if they show any signs of prolonged unhappiness.

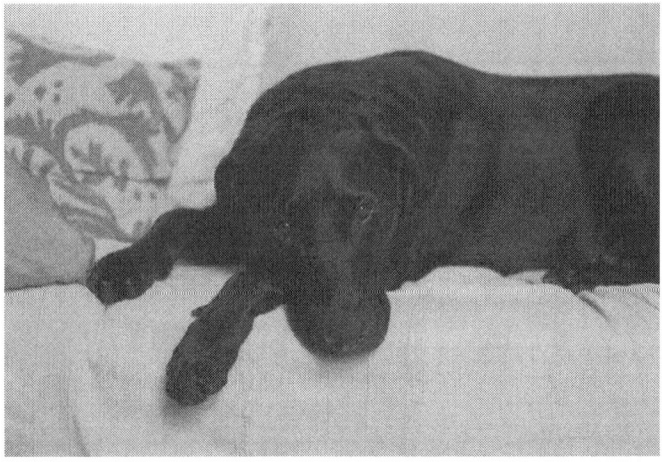

Sad Black Lab

What Is Aggression in Dogs?

Aggression in dogs is something many people struggle to understand because it's something we never learn how to deal with. The vast majority of aggression that happens in dogs is caused by one of three things: frustration, stress, or fear.

Keep in mind, any dog can be aggressive. It's not something specific to certain breeds or even certain households. Sure, a dog that grows up stray or in a hostile environment is definitely more prone to aggression, but even the most placid household pet can lash out if it is put in a compromised situation. Aggression in dogs is not premeditated. Humans have the ability to plan out and think about what they do long beforehand; dogs can't do this, and so, any aggression they show is done on instinct and impulse.

At the end of the day, aggression in dogs comes down to humans misreading or ignoring signals, or one of the two dogs involved being inexperienced in social situations.

Teeth Bared

Chapter 2: Types of Canine Aggression

I've seen happy families turned into anxious, wrecked households by uncontrolled dog behavioral problems. It's not just worrying about your dog barking too much and annoying the neighbors, or coming home to find that your favorite cushion has been ripped to pieces. It's the fear that the next time you have guests over, someone gets bitten, or the next time you take a trip to the dog park, another pet gets hurt. It can absolutely destroy your ability to enjoy being around your pet.

Dog aggression is a serious problem, but it's luckily one that can be corrected and managed with the right techniques and enough effort.

Protective Aggression

Protective aggression is a very widespread form of aggression that I've dealt with plenty of times throughout the years. This type of aggression is characterized by significant hostility towards anyone or anything that is perceived as a threat to their owner or pack. This can be caused by a traumatic experience, past abuse, or a lack of social skills. For example, an adopted dog may show aggression toward men with long beards after seeing a man with a long beard "threaten" their family. Keep in mind this is all up to the animal's interpretation; that bearded man could have been throwing a water-balloon at a birthday party for all we know.

Maternal Aggression

Maternal aggression is a common form of aggression in female dogs and mothers with new litters of puppies. This aggression is usually caused by the mother dog interpreting something, or someone, as a threat to her litter and subsequently lashing out at that threat. While this tends to be hormonal and short-lived, it may turn into a learned behavior that will last long after her pups have been weaned. In more uncommon cases, maternal aggression may be present in female dogs that view small children as a member of their pack; however, this treads the line between protective aggression and maternal aggression.

Protective Mother

Territorial Aggression

Territorial aggression (also known as guard dog aggression) is a form of aggression centered around the dog's believed "territory." This form of aggression is displayed towards other dogs and humans most and is arguably the most common form of aggression we may see. Dogs showing this type of aggression are typically completely passive outside of their "territory" but become aggressive and combative when approached inside their territory by an outsider. This "territory" is typically an owner's home or yard but can extend to an area beyond that. Dogs with this form of aggression can be very dangerous if antagonized and can often harass or injure city workers such as postmen and waste disposal workers.

Under the Gate

Irritable or Pain Aggression

This is a form of aggression I'm sure we can all relate to. Irritable and pain aggressions are caused by discomfort, pain, or something else that is making your pet feel unwell. These feelings of pain and discomfort can make your pet feel vulnerable or scared, which in turn, may manifest as aggression. A wounded animal is always at its most dangerous, and even if Fido has never shown so much as an aggressive sneeze in his life, he may lash out when in pain or discomfort. If your pet has suddenly started showing aggression with no prior hints or history, have your vet examine them and check for underlying medical problems.

Predatory Aggression

Predatory aggression is a form of aggression that is common in herding and hunting breeds. These breeds have a natural disposition to chasing prey animals. In a home, this may be triggered by mice; I more often see this aggression triggered by squirrels, raccoons, and other wild suburban animals. In rare cases, you might see this type of aggression caused by fast-moving peoples or objects that trigger our pet's predatory instinct. For example, vehicles, joggers, bicycles, skateboards, remote-controlled toys, and other pets like cats.

Sexual Aggression

This is far less common in neutered (both female and male) dogs but can be common in unneutered animals around periods of mating. Male dogs may show significant aggression towards other male dogs and male humans when there is competition for a female partner that is in heat. Female dogs may also show aggression towards other female dogs and humans when there is competition for male partners. This type of aggression is often easily corrected by neutering the problem animal, but as with all behavior, it can become learned over time.

Frustration Aggression

Frustration aggression is another very common form of aggression I see all too often. This type of aggression can stem from improper leash training, the frustration of being in confined spaces, or too much pent-up energy. Many dogs without proper leash training may lash out when placed on a leash because they feel confined and are frustrated with not being able to act how they want. Similarly, some dogs may get frustrated being kept in a small space, like an apartment or a small yard. Many breeds need to be able to run and get frequent exercise, and when this is denied to them, they may become anxious and frustrated.

Sibling Aggression

Sibling aggression is a form of dog-to-dog social aggression that can affect multi-dog households. This form of aggression is brought on by conflict or escalation of "play fighting" that leads to one party being aggravated and subsequently lashing out at the other. We often see this between young dogs or dogs clumsy in social environments. They may engage in playful behavior with other dogs, only to take the playing too far, act too roughly, or attempt to dominate the other dog. This type of aggression is also occasionally directed towards humans the dog may be playing with and can manifest in bites and scratches that hurt the human but come across as playful to the dog.

Disease-Related Aggression

Disease-related aggression is the rarest and scariest type of dog aggression you may run into. Of course, when people think of diseases that cause aggression, they think of rabies. Luckily, the rabies vaccination is mandatory for all dogs over four months that visit a vet in the United States. Because of the widespread campaign against rabies by the CDC over the last few decades, rabies cases in dogs have dropped down to 63 in 2018. This means out of the 90 million dogs in the USA, yours have a 0.00007 percent chance of catching rabies.

Some other more common (but still rare) causes of disease-related aggression are hyperthyroidism, canine cognitive dysfunction (canine dementia), and epilepsy.

Dog Aggressions Management

If your dog displays aggression and symptoms of any of these diseases, I would recommend immediately taking them to a vet and having a full blood panel done to rule out or diagnose any diseases that may be the cause of erratic behavior. Many of these diseases are manageable or even treatable.

Anxiety or Fear Aggression

Fear and anxiety aggressions are the single most common reasons for domestic dogs to show aggression, even in the most loving households. Many types of aggression already have a fear or anxiety component, but they can have complex triggers or socio-hierarchical implications. In its most basic form, fear and anxiety aggressions are caused by your pet feeling scared and needing to protect itself from a perceived threat. This is a manifestation of the fight or flight reflex. This aggression is often misinterpreted because lunging and barking may come across as aggressive body language. When, in actual fact, this combative and hostile behavior is just a defensive reflex to something your pet is scared of.

Golden Snarl

Dominance Aggression

Dominance aggression is another dog-to-dog aggression that focuses on the social hierarchies that are formed in the packs of domestic dogs. Just like their wolf cousins, domestic dogs are pack animals that have strict social structures. One dog may be lower in the hierarchy than another, and if that dominant dog ever feels like the lower animal is challenging them or posing a threat to their position, they often won't hesitate to try to put them back in their place. This type of aggression is especially common in multi-dog households with multiple males. Older males, especially, may feel the need to put younger dogs in their place, and if there are females involved, then we may even cross the line into sexual aggression providing some of the parties aren't neutered.

Idiopathic Aggression

Idiopathic aggression is the least understood out of all the types of aggression mentioned here. It's completely unpredictable and we have no idea what the triggers may be. We don't really know enough about mental illness in dogs to properly diagnose or treat idiopathic aggression. Even the word "idiopathic" denotes the randomness of this type of aggression, "relating to or denoting any disease or condition which arises spontaneously or for which the cause is unknown" (Lexico, n.d.). This aggression can be incredibly dangerous because there is no way to tell when an outburst may occur and how severe it may be. Because of this, treatment options are also very limited.

Genetic Aggression

Lastly, genetic aggression. I'm sure you've heard that certain breeds like pit bulls or Rottweilers are genetically predisposed to aggression. Well, this is completely untrue, a myth. In a study by the School of Veterinary Science at Bristol University, the results showed that the breed of dog is a negligible factor in the chances of that animal displaying aggression. The animal's home environment, place of adoption, age, sex, neuter status, and history of training all have more impactful roles in whether an animal can become aggressive or not (Casey et al., 2014).

Things That Can Cause Aggression

As we just covered, there are quite a few different types of aggression and each type potentially has its own quirks in how we are meant to prevent it and fix it. Despite there being so many types of aggression, many of them boil down to a few simple causes. All of these causes are intrinsically linked to anxiety and stress, but they all contribute massively to building the stress that will lead to aggression in our dogs.

Frustration

Frustration can both lead to its own type of aggression and other types. Dogs can get frustrated by quite a few things in life, but luckily, the signs of frustration are easy to spot. Dogs are incredibly curious creatures, they are incredibly playful and sociable, and they feel the need for a purpose. See, almost all breeds of dogs have been bred with a specific job in mind, whether that be herding, hunting, guarding, birding, or one of the other many generational jobs that dogs have been bred for over the centuries. Because of this, your dog can get very frustrated if they don't have anything to do. Similar to how people can get cabin fever from being inside, alone, and without any stimulation for too long, dogs can also get very angsty.

Arousal

Arousal in dogs is classified as a physical and psychological state of alertness and readiness. This leads to an increased heart rate, high blood pressure, tense muscles, and an increase of adrenaline. Arousal in dogs is quite simply their way of being alert and reactive to their environment. This is a common state for many dogs to experience but for some dogs, it happens in excess or higher levels of intensity. These prolonged and higher levels of arousal can lead to severe anxiety and hysteria in dogs.

In some dogs, the arousal levels get intense to the extent that the dog struggles to contain itself, which interferes with their ability to think clearly. Levels of arousal like this may be the reason your dog will be barking at cars passing by one second, then fighting at the fence with the neighbor's pets the next. Your dog is just excited and looking for a way to express this excitement, even though in that moment, the excitement is causing them to act out in potentially troublesome ways.

Dog Aggressions Management

Conflict

A common trigger for aggression in dogs is witnessing conflict elsewhere. Dogs are family animals and will often do anything to come to the defense of their family. Because of this, perceived conflict between other dogs or humans can cause the protective side of your dog to trigger. For example, if two of your older dogs are play-fighting, your younger, less experienced dog may misinterpret it as actual fighting and aggressively involve themselves in the fight. Similarly, if a dog's humans are arguing, play-fighting, or even displaying signs that may come across as aggressive like raising voices, your dog may take that as a cue to come to your rescue and aggressively intervene.

Entrapment

Entrapment is a very common issue with larger breeds of dogs. Many dogs, especially your larger breeds, naturally need a lot of exercise and space. If you try to keep a Siberian husky in a tiny courtyard, you are going to have a dog that feels trapped and claustrophobic. Dogs, like many animals, naturally want to be able to roam, explore, and exercise. Without being able to do that, your dog may become depressed, agitated, and frustrated. This can apply to some smaller breeds of dogs too, especially many terrier breeds who are naturally very energetic and inquisitive. A Jack Russel that never goes on walks and doesn't have a space to exercise and play will become a problematic animal as they search for other ways to release their pent-up energy.

Chapter 3: Is All Aggression Bad?

The simple answer is, yes. But, some of the early warning signs of aggression are actually a blessing. Unlike people who can hide their intentions, dogs show a clear pattern of escalation and give constant warnings every step of the way. So, although all aggression is bad, all aggression is avoidable and forewarned.

Clients and students of mine in the past have always looked a bit bewildered when I've told them that the early signs of aggression that dogs show are a good thing. Many people have grown up with a corporal punishment mindset when dealing with their pets, "Oh, Fido growled at the children pulling his hair? Time to smack Fido with a slipper." This is possibly the worst way to handle early signs of aggression.

It may seem perfectly reasonable to punish a dog that is showing this kind of behavior. Growling leads to snapping, snapping leads to biting, biting leads to Fido being euthanized as a problem animal. So many people will pick the lesser of two evils and beat Fido if he shows any aggression. If you understand canine behavior, you'll realize just how counterintuitive this is.

For most animals, dogs included, fighting is the very last resort. Every instinct yells self-preservation, which usually means run, hide, or scare the threat off. The signals that we see leading up to aggression are meant to ward us off and tell us that we need to leave them alone. A dog that doesn't want to fight is going to bark, growl, lunge, hide, and do anything else in its power to avoid it.

Typically, a dog will start with subtle signals of being uncomfortable or anxious that are very easy for the unaware to overlook. These signs can be tense body movements, anxious low tail wagging, a wide-eyed stare, or any number of other signals. These are the dog's way of saying "Please leave me alone, I'm not comfortable."

Continuing to ignore a dog's boundaries and invade their personal space can lead to an escalation in their threats. These could be freezing in place, a snarl, or their ears being pressed back against their head, among other signs. This means "Hey! Back off, I mean it."

Dog Aggressions Management

If we continue to disregard the warnings presented to us, a dog may resort to snapping, a lite nip, or other physical contacts like scratching. This is a final "don't make me bite you" warning.

If the human *still* doesn't get the message, then the dog may feel like it needs to bite harder, possibly enough to break the skin. At this stage, the dog feels like this is the only way they can protect themselves, their territory, their pack, or their possessions.

Aggression in people can stem from any number of different sources, but with dogs, it always comes from stress. Sometimes, it's good stress like excitement, but most of the time, it's from anxiety, fear, pain, or perceived threats. A confrontational, aggressive dog may attack because another dog or human has trespassed into its territory. A scared dog will bite because it is scared and wants to defend itself. A dog in pain may bite the hand of a rescuer or vet because it is confused and stressed by how vulnerable it feels. A mother dog may lunge and bite because she feels that her puppies are threatened and she wants to protect them. Every single action has a clear and avoidable root motive.

When dealing with a dog that is showing early signs of any kind of aggression, you need to make sure you address it properly. You have to approach these signs in a way that doesn't encourage or reinforce the behavior you want to correct. If you punish a dog that is snapping, you may succeed at stopping that behavior but you don't remove the cause of their stress. If anything, you make them more stressed by making yourself a bad guy in their eyes. Instead of respecting a dog's boundaries, you overstep and punish them. This just reinforces that they have something to be afraid of.

By punishing a stressed dog, and forcing it to hide warning signs, we create an unpredictable animal that can bite without clear warning.

Let's say Fido always barks at the doorbell; every time he does it, you shout "No, bad dog!" You may think, "This is what every good owner should do; my neighbors don't want to hear my dog barking and my guests don't want to be barked at." So, every time the doorbell rings, Fido barks, and Fido gets punished. Fido doesn't learn that the doorbell isn't a threat; in fact, Fido learns that the doorbell ringing *is* bad because he always gets punished when it rings. He learns that not only does the doorbell cause more stress, but it makes you mad when he barks at it. So, Fido becomes more stressed by the doorbell but also barks less at it.

Dog Aggressions Management

You think, "Well, he's learned his lesson. He no longer barks at the doorbell."

Now next time you have guests over and the doorbell rings, instead of holding back a barking Fido, you let him approach the door. Fido is even more stressed than usual. He's already stressed because of the doorbell but now he has to hide that stress from you. He also smells unfamiliar people on the other side of the door.

When that door opens and the first person comes inside his territory so suddenly, Fido feels nothing but total fear and anxiety. "We're being attacked in our own home!" he thinks. Fido then lunges at this doorbell-ringing person; he snaps at them but you're able to hold him back before anyone is bitten.

Fido is terrified, your guests are shaken, and you are in disbelief; "I thought he was behaving better," you say to yourself and your guests.

I can't tell you how many times I've heard a story like this told by clients. A dog's warning signs are their way of asking for help. You wouldn't punish a scared child for calling for help, so treat your dogs with the same care and respect.

Chapter 4: Does Neutering Help?

The debate whether neutering is worth it or not has been raging for decades. In North America, neutering is the default for most dogs. In Europe though, neutering is far less common. A study in Sweden found that 99 percent of dogs in their sample weren't neutered. A Hungarian survey revealed that 57 percent of dogs were unneutered, and a study in Great Britain showed that 46 percent of dogs were fully intact. In Norway, it is actually illegal to neuter your pet unless you have a valid reason that has been confirmed by a qualified veterinary specialist.

Before going any further, I thought we should clarify something. The term "neutering" is often used incorrectly to only mean male dogs. In fact, neutering applies to both male and female dogs. The term specific to males is castration and the term specific to females is spaying. In both cases, neutering refers to the removal of reproductive organs, whether they be the ovaries, uterus, or testicles.

Why Should I Neuter?

Preventing Unwanted Pregnancies

According to the American Kennel Club's chief veterinary officer, Dr. Jerry Klein, there are some very convincing reasons to neuter your dog. Possibly the best reason to neuter your female dog would be to avoid unwanted puppies. An unneutered female will come into "heat" for a few weeks every year. During this time, she will be irresistible to male dogs who may be able to smell her from miles around. This can bring plenty of unwanted visitors to your doorstep, which may be very problematic, especially if your female isn't the only dog in the household. Having a litter of puppies can be very costly for the dog's owner too. Your bitch will need veterinary check-ups during the pregnancy, the delivery may involve very expensive surgery, and it may result in the loss of the children or mother.

Once the litter is born, each pup will need to have a veterinary check-up and mandatory shots. Then comes the issue of finding good homes for puppies, which can be a big challenge, unless you want to keep them (but this is also added expenses).

Neutering is the best and most foolproof way of avoiding unwanted puppies. Dog breeding should be left to responsible and accredited professional breeders. Expert breeders have a detailed idea of the genetic history of their dogs so as to avoid animals that may suffer from diseases or disabilities in life.

Effects on Behavior

As we mentioned above, male dogs may end up roaming for miles to find female partners in heat. This can be very dangerous for dogs in any environment, but especially for urban or suburban animals. Some vets also recommend neutering to help with behavioral issues. This is a hotly contested topic, although there is evidence that neutering can help limit behaviors like leg-lifting and mounting. The evidence on whether neutering helps limit aggression has been swaying negatively in the last few years.

Reducing Health Risks

Neutering your pets can have a profound effect on their later-in-life health. Unneutered females may suffer from a very serious form of uterus infection called pyometra. This infection can be life-threatening and very costly to treat. Around 50% of unneutered female dogs will suffer from breast or uterine tumors. By spaying your pet before her first heat, you can drastically decrease the chances of these tumors forming.

Neutering male dogs can dramatically decrease their chances of developing testicular cancer or prostate diseases later in life. On top of that, neutered dogs are less likely to injure themselves trying to find a partner. An unneutered dog will do just about anything to find a mate when the mood hits them; this can include finding dangerous ways to escape home, crossing miles of a dangerous urban jungle, and fighting other dogs.

What Age Should We Neuter?

Dogs should typically be neutered under nine months. Healthy pups can be neutered at as young as eight weeks, providing they are healthy. Worryingly though, studies show that although the age of neutering does not affect males, females who are neutered before one year of age show a considerable increase in aggression compared to later neutering.

Research funded by the American Kennel Club's Canine Health Foundation has found that there may be great benefits to neutering dogs only *after* puberty. These benefits can include a reduction in many cancers, a lower chance of orthopedic health issues, and a reduction in hormonal problems.

Dog Aggressions Management

Post-Op Cone

Why Shouldn't I Neuter?

Although there are some very valid reasons for neutering your pets, there is an ever-increasing amount of evidence that suggests it may not be the best decision for your dog's well-being.

How valid is this evidence? Do the reasons to not neuter your pets outweigh the reasons to neuter them? According to a treatise written by Laura J. Sanborn M.S., in which she examined over 50 peer-reviewed papers and assessed the health impacts that are caused by neutering, the evidence may side with not neutering your pets (Sanborn and Katz, 2007).

Behavior Changes

In a study by the School of Veterinary Medicine at the University of Pennsylvania, two separate sample groups of 1,552 dogs and 3,593 dogs showed that aggression was drastically increased for dogs that were neutered. Depending on the type of aggression, the increase was anything from as low as 20 percent to as high as double the level of aggression. These results were similar for males and females (Duffy and Serpell, 2006).

Another unsettling finding from this study was that neutered dogs displayed a 31 percent increase in fearful behavior in both sexes, meaning they were more prone to anxiety. A 33 percent increase in touch sensitivity was also observed in these dogs, meaning they were more fearful when being touched and more likely to lash out at strangers touching them.

Hormonal Processes

Although the recommended age of neutering is before nine months, it has been shown through a retroactive study that this may be too young. Dogs that are neutered before their first year are likely to suffer from improper hormonal processes. The sexual organs are the primary source of hormones, and although removing them will stop sexual activity, it may also impact the growth and maturation of your pets.

Hormonal disruption in male dogs has also been shown to increase the chances of hypothyroidism by as much as three times.

Increase in Cancer Risk

While neutering may help decrease the chances of testicular and uterine cancers, it greatly increases the chances of bone cancer (osteosarcoma) in both male and female dogs by at least two times.

Neutered dogs also show a two times more likely risk of developing urinary tract cancers. These cancers manifest in tumors around or inside the bladder and urethra. These tumors are almost always malignant but only make up around one percent of canine tumors.

Hemangiosarcoma is a cancer that affects the blood vessel walls and is common in many breeds of dogs. It is a chief noted cause of death in golden retrievers, bulldogs, German shepherds, Boxers, Afghan hounds, Scottish terriers, Boston terriers, Irish water spaniels, and salukis. A retrospective study on cases of this cancer has shown that female dogs have a greater than five times risk of developing this cancer if spayed. Male dogs have nearly a two times greater risk of developing this cancer if they are neutered.

Obesity

Because of changes in metabolism, neutering can have strong negative effects on the weight of your dog. A study performed by the Faculty of Veterinary Science at the University of Sydney, Australia, found that neutered animals were one and a half times (females) and three times (males) more likely to become obese than dogs that hadn't been neutered. As with people, obesity in dogs is a serious issue and can lead to many health problems, some life-threatening.

Obese Dog

Hip Dysplasia and Orthopedic Disorders

Neutering before the age of six months has shown as much as a 70 percent increase in the risk of a dog developing hip dysplasia. This is due to the neutering process delaying the closure of growth plates in the bones around the pelvis and lower spine. Neutering done during the closing of growth plates may lead to your dog developing unusual proportions around their hindquarters. This can lead to serious wear of the joints and cartilage in the pelvis, legs, and spine.

Part 2: Observing and Communicating

Chapter 5: Identifying Dog Calming and Stress Signals

Whenever I'm anxious, I tend to pull on my clothes; I can't count the number of loose collars and stretched sleeves I've made over the years. When my partner is trying to help calm me down, they rub my arm a lot. My dog always scratches himself when he's nervous. These are calming signals, also known as stress signals, and pretty much every living creature has them.

What Is a Calming/Stress Signal?

The terms "calming signal" and "stress signal" may sound counter-intuitive but they do actually stand for the same thing. These are signals we display both when we are stressed and when we need to calm ourselves, as a coping mechanism.

Dog Aggressions Management

The term "calming signal" was originally coined by legendary dog trainer and behaviorist Turid Rugaas and has become a recognized term around the world by trainers and experts.

It is believed that there are three main categories of calming signals used by dogs: visual, olfactory, and auditory. Visual is displayed by various aggressive, fearful, or submissive acts. Olfactory signals are characterized by the use of pheromones and territory marking. And, auditory signals come in the form of sounds like barking, growling, snapping, etc.

Why Do Dogs Use These Signals?

Calming signals are a key part of communication between dogs. These signals act as the first line of defense against aggression from other dogs or anything your pet may be afraid of. These signals are, in their most basic form, a set of body language cues that help dogs protect against conflict and help them keep healthy relationships without the use of aggression.

Typically, we will see these actions very early in interactions. As soon as your dog realizes the other dog may be on edge or nervous, expect to see various calming signals being used to relax the situation. Not only are these signs used to help calm your dog and other dogs they meet, but they can also be used to simply be welcoming and work as a greeting.

Dogs that lack proper social skills, i.e., they are raised without frequent contact with other dogs, may suffer and find themselves unable to properly respond to or reciprocate calming signals. This can lead to aggression, which can become a learned behavior for those dogs.

Just like how people might shake hands and exchange a smile to show they mean no harm, dogs will exchange calming signals to each other and humans for the same reason.

What to Look for and How to Respond?

Examples of Calming Signals

- **Barking and Whining**: Barking and whining are the most common form of calming signals we will come across. Barking is used by dogs to display aggression, fear, anxiety, and excitement. A scared or aggressive dog may bark as a warning to "stay away," and an anxious or excited dog may bark or whine to get our attention.

- **Shaking**: I'm sure you've seen your dog shaking off the water in their fur after they've been out in the rain, often in your living room to your dismay. Similarly, I'm sure you've seen your pet do that same shake when being put down from the vet's table or after interacting with another dog. This "shaking off" is a common stress sign for dogs that can show they are uncomfortable at that moment in time.

- **Pacing**: Just like humans, dogs also pace when they are stressed. You may see your dog pace the same path around you at the park or follow the same route around the vet's exam room.

- **Yawning**: Another thing dogs and humans

share in common is the anxiety yawn. When they're anxious, their heart rate goes up, and because of this, their body needs more air. This can lead to long and intense yawns.

Nervous Yawn

- **Drooling and Licking**: Dogs may also drool and lick excessively when they are nervous. The licking is seen as a sign of friendliness and submission. Because of the increase in mouth movement due to licking or yawning, excessive saliva may be created, which leads to drooling.
- **Panting**: Similar to yawning, a dog may pant when nervous due to the increase in heart rate and body temperature. If you notice that your dog is panting even though they haven't

moved around much and the room temperature is fine, then they may be feeling stressed or anxious.

Panting Dog

- **Eye Signals**: Dogs that are nervous or anxious may have various calming signals that they communicate with their eyes. A stressed dog may blink their eyes rapidly or have very dilated pupils. They also may open their eyes very wide; if you can see the whites of a dog's eyes that typically means they are nervous or afraid.

- **Ear Signals**: Ear signals are another very common form of signal communication. If your dog has its ears pinned back against its head or flattened backward, then that is a sure sign of its discomfort and anxiety.

- **Shedding**: Dogs shed a lot when nervous. It's a common phenomenon for show dogs to "blow their coat" when in front of a large crowd. You may also notice a lot of hair on the inside of their carrier or on car upholstery after a drive. This is less noticeable in outdoor settings, but even at the dog park, your pet may be anxiety shedding.

- **Urination**: Just like some people, some dogs can feel the need to go to the restroom when they are particularly nervous or anxious. For dogs, peeing when nervous can be a submissive signal of appeasement. It can also act as territory marking, a sort of "I'm nervous, please don't come into my space."

- **Avoidance**: Avoidance is another very common form of calm signaling from dogs. If you have visitors over, for example, your dog may avoid them and sniff the ground, clean themselves, or distract themselves with a toy. This comes across as an "If I ignore them, they will ignore me" signal.

- **Escaping**: An extension on avoidance, escaping is when your dog decides that it wants to escape to another room or hide behind you or a piece of furniture when it is nervous. Your dog may also try to force you to leave with them by nudging you or performing diversions like circling around you or digging.

Hiding Dog

- **Bowing**: I'm sure you've seen dogs doing that playful bow that they do. That is often a calming signal that one dog may do to another to calm the mood. Either your dog or the other dog may be stressed or nervous, so the more confident of the two will bow to show appeasement and invite the other to play.
- **Splitting**: Splitting is a common behavior that we will see when multiple dogs or people are grouped together. If a dog perceives tension between two other dogs or two other humans, it may try to put itself between the two

parties.

- **Tail Wagging**: Wagging tails are often seen as a sign of happiness, but often a wagging tail can also show anxiety and fear. If your dog is slinking down low, laying with its head down, or showing submission in any other way while wagging its tail, this means it is nervous and trying to show that it is not a threat.

Wagging Tail

- **Freezing**: Just like a scared deer may freeze in the headlights of a car, a scared dog may also freeze when presented with something that scares them. This behavior particularly happens when the thing they are scared of catches them off guard, is very loud, or very large.

- **Curving**: When dogs curve, they approach other dogs in a curved motion rather than head-on. Approaching head-on can be seen as antagonistic behavior and can result in aggression, so whenever possible, dogs will try to approach from the side and curve around each other.

- **Fiddling or Playing**: Lastly, many dogs will approach a scared or anxious dog by jumping around, throwing sticks and toys, and just acting silly in general. This is meant to show that they are not a threat and are open to playing with the other dog. Although it doesn't look calming, it actually does have a calming effect.

How to Respond to Calming/Stress Signals

If your dog displays calming signals, you must first try to figure out what it is that is causing them stress. Is it something in their environment? Is it another dog? Is it you?

Dog Aggressions Management

Figuring out what causes them stress simply comes down to observing them during the day, taking note of when they exhibit calming signals, and noting what happened at that time that could have caused them stress. For example, did the neighbor decide to mow their lawn, and now your pet is panting and hiding behind the sofa? In this situation, we know that it's a good chance the lawnmower is the cause of our pets' anxiety.

In that case, we should try to put our pet in a quiet room away from the stress-causing noise. Once away from the noise, we should try to introduce something normal to our pet. If you usually use one specific toy from playing with them, give it to them. If your pet is trained in sitting or heeling, you can give them a command and reward them for successfully performing it. This can be incredibly comforting to a scared pet.

Part 3: Corrective Actions

Chapter 6: What Can We Do to Help?

Taking note of everything we have learned up until this point, our first move when looking to help our pet is always to observe. Figure out what causes our pet stress and then move them away from it, or move yourself away from them. Make sure you have a clear idea of the cause of their stress before doing anything.

Always keep your cool; our pets take a lot of emotional cues from us. If we seem stressed, they will feed off of that and become more stressed too. If you've figured out that something you were doing caused these initial warning signs, stop doing it. This could be anything from vacuuming the lounge to hugging your pet too tightly. Yes, this may teach your pet that growling or barking gets you to stop something, but this small reinforcement will be overwritten down the line through training. Right now, it's important to just limit the stress your pet feels.

Once you have the causes of your pet's stress noted down, you can start looking at what behavioral development techniques you need to take your dog through to help correct their behavior.

From my experience, I've found that counterconditioning and desensitization work brilliantly hand-in-hand to correct nearly every stress-based behavioral issue your pet may display.

Desensitization

Desensitization means slowly and gradually introducing your pet to the thing that stresses and scares them. With desensitization, you need to start off at a very low level, and very slowly build up. This isn't a process of a few days; this is a process of a few months. At every step of the process, you need to make sure your dog is safe and happy.

If at any point you notice your dog displaying signs of stress or discomfort, even a tiny amount, you need to immediately stop and wait for the next session to try that level of exposure again. If you rush your dog and introduce their fears too fast, you risk making them more sensitive and scared, achieving the opposite of what we want.

For example, an issue my clients often have is their pet being terrified by fireworks. One way we may desensitize our pet to these sounds is by playing them at a low volume. If the dog reacts well and doesn't show any adverse reactions, you can reward them and then try increasing the volume a tiny bit the following day. Repeat this until the sound is being played at normal volume and your dog isn't showing signs of anxiety or stress. Assuming you don't rush the process and your dog is receptive to the training, it will learn to tolerate the noises, which make them stressed.

Counterconditioning

Counterconditioning is a form of dog conditioning that stems directly from Ivan Pavlov and his dogs. If you don't know about Pavlov, he was a Russian physiologist whose research is credited as being the foundation for the psychological school of behaviorism. Pavlov, in his experiments relating to digestion, noted that in the presence of the technician that fed them, his dogs would produce more saliva.

Dog Aggressions Management

He expanded upon this by isolating the stimuli in his experiments.

He knew that the dogs would always salivate more in the presence of food; this made the food the natural *unconditioned stimulus*. This meant the dogs needed no conditioning to react this way. Pavlov then presented the dogs with a metronome. This metronome meant nothing to the dogs at first; it was a *neutral stimulus*.

Pavlov then presented the metronome and the food to the dogs at the same time over the course of multiple meals. Soon enough, the dogs would start to associate the introduction of the metronome with food coming. This meant the metronome changed from a *neutral stimulus* to a *conditioned stimulus*. And, the dog's reaction to the metronome became a *conditioned response*. He took something completely unrelated to food and conditioned the dogs into associating it with food whenever they saw it.

The Pavlov experiment above describes classical conditioning. Counterconditioning differs in that we will take a negative stimulus (e.g., fireworks), and every time that stimulus frightens our dog, we will present them with a positive stimulus (e.g., food or a treat). The idea is that we take a bad thing and make it not bad by introducing something better to our dogs when it happens. Fireworks may be scary, but a piece of chicken is so nice that it takes their attention away from the fireworks, and so, your dog will start to associate fireworks with chicken and, therefore, be less afraid when fireworks happen.

For this type of conditioning to be effective, you need to make sure that you are able to *always* reply with treats when your dog is presented with its trigger. So, if the trigger you are trying to help your dog cope with is a very common one (e.g., other dogs, car horns, etc.), you need to make sure you always have treats on hand; otherwise, you risk undoing hours of work.

Award-winning author and dog trainer Jean Donaldson developed the *open bar/closed bar* technique as an extension of counterconditioning. This technique takes our giving of treats when a trigger appears and turns it up a notch.

When practicing this technique, instead of giving treats on a one-to-one ratio, when the trigger shows itself, the bar opens. This means we give multiple treats until the trigger goes away. This keeps our pet's attention on the positive treats and teaches them that when that trigger shows up *really* good things happen.

Using Desensitization and Counterconditioning Together

These two techniques work incredibly well hand-in-hand. By both desensitizing our pets to the trigger and making them associate the trigger with something positive, we are improving their reaction on two fronts.

Keeping with our example of a dog that is afraid of fireworks, we can desensitize them by repeatedly playing gradually louder fireworks sounds to them over the course of a few weeks.

While we do this, we will also counter-condition them to expect treats whenever they hear fireworks. This combination of methods is incredibly effective and can help your pet overcome any triggers they may have.

Common Mistakes

There are quite a few common errors we can make while trying to effectively implement desensitization and counterconditioning. If you're worried about making mistakes in your first attempt or failed a previous attempt, check if any of these may apply to you.

Not Properly Reading Body Language

Counterconditioning and desensitization are as much a learning exercise for your pet as it is for you. The most difficult skill you will learn during the process is being able to read your dog's body language. There are dozens of subtle cues your pet will give off during times of stress and anxiety, and being able to read these cues is incredibly important. Far too many people don't put the necessary time into working on and improving their ability to read the subtle signals their pet puts out.

Being able to read their behavior is also key for being able to notice positive responses to exercises. You want to be able to tell what you're doing is working so you can move on to the next step.

Moving Too Fast

Trying to progress too quickly is probably the most common mistake people make when trying to correct bad behavior in their pets. When practicing desensitization and counterconditioning, we have to move at the dog's pace. Each dog may have a different speed at which they learn; some are more timid than others, some learn faster, some slower. Patience is crucial regardless.

There are many signs that you may be moving too fast, but some obvious ones include your dog being tense when taking treats (e.g., snapping, hard mouth), being disinterested in treats or rewards, and anxious body language like a low tail, scared eyes, and panting. If your dog shows any of these signs, go back to an easier stage of its training.

Not Using Enough Incentive

We all know how picky our pets can be. When training your dog, especially with this type of in-depth conditioning, you are relying on your incentives to change the way your dog perceives things. The treats you use must be exactly the things your dog loves. If your dog loves a particular brand of doggy treat, make sure to use that. Maybe your dog has loved chicken since it was a puppy or maybe cheese really gets them excited. Whatever it may be, make sure your pet absolutely loves it and it is safe for them to consume.

Doggy Treats

Mixing up Your Timings

Remember the order of things in counterconditioning. You want to use food to *counter* the effects of whatever scares your pet. This means you need to introduce the scary thing and then introduce the treat. If you start seeing that your dog gets anxious after receiving treats, then you've probably conditioned them to expect bad things after getting treats, and not the other way around.

This is a simple thing to avoid though. It all comes down to paying attention and understanding body language cues again. Once you see that your dog is anxious, you feed them. Don't give your pet anything until you are sure they are anxious.

Using the Wrong Tools

There are only two tools you need when doing counterconditioning and desensitization. You need your dog treats and whatever your pet is scared of. That's it.

Sure, clickers and target sticks have their uses in other forms of training, and they can be very effective there. But, with these two methods of behavioral development, any other tools will do nothing but make things more complicated for you and your pet.

Other Options

As effective as desensitization and counterconditioning are, you may find that other techniques are needed to help with certain dogs or certain issues that they face.

Response Substitution

Response substitution is one of these alternative techniques that has shown to also be very effective in changing behaviors in our dogs. This technique takes an undesirable response to a stimulus and changes it into a desirable response. When practicing this technique, it's important to only reward positive responses.

Dog Aggressions Management

For example, let's say your dog is scared of car horns. Instead of your dog trying to run and hide whenever they hear a car horn, you want to train them to respond differently. In this situation, you may want to train your dog to lay down or sit. You want to teach your dog that running and hiding doesn't earn them anything, but if they lay down or sit, they will get a treat from you. We substitute a negative response with a positive one.

This form of training is very effective when paired with desensitization. The end goal of this training is not only to replace the negative response with a positive one but to also make sure our dog is focused, calm, and happy when executing that response.

Sticking with the car horn example. If you want to include desensitization with your training, you would train your pet how to sit or lay down. Once they are performing that comfortably and happily, you will add in the negative stimulus. You would add in this stimulus in the form of softly playing car horn recordings. Just like with the desensitization above, you must monitor your pet carefully to make sure they aren't frightened.

With the sounds playing, try to have your pet perform the sit or lay down commands. Reward them if they perform the commands, even if they need some encouragement. If your pet manages to perform the command, then you can look to increase the volume of the stimulus next time. Continue increasing the difficulty until your pet is comfortable performing the commands at a real-world volume.

Gentle Touch

Operant Conditioning

Operant conditioning is a technique based on teaching your dog to not perform a certain behavior by showing them the consequences of that behavior. There are four types of behavior-to-consequence relationships you may run into when using this form of training. Those are positive and negative punishment and positive and negative reinforcement. Reinforcement increases the chances that a behavior will be repeated in the future. Punishment leads to a reduction in future behavior. Negative means the removal of a stimulus, while positive means adding a stimulus.

Positive punishment happens when a behavior decreases in frequency or intensity after the application of a stimulus, usually something unpleasant. **Negative punishment** happens when a behavior decreases in frequency or in intensity after the removal of a stimulus, normally something nice and appealing.

When concerning positive punishment, if the behavior you are trying to correct does not decrease after the initial few sessions, then the punishment is either not being properly timed or the behavior you are trying to correct is too deeply set or strongly motivated to be reduced by punishment. Positive punishment that is performed by an owner or trainer is meant to cause the pet to become fearful of repeating the behavior. This, of course, has the consequence that your pet may start to associate you or the trainer with the punishment and, therefore, become fearful of you. This may just reinforce your pet's fears. Another potential unwanted consequence of this training method could be that your dog learns to only react badly when you are not around. This could lead to issues with your pet being left alone or with others.

Positive punishment paired with the introduction of a stimulus can create a more conditioned fear of the stimulus. For example, if you are trying to train your dog to not bark at cars by spraying them with water whenever they do, you might just reinforce their fear by showing them that bad things always happen when cars are around.

Keep in mind, punishment will never work in encouraging good behaviors, only in preventing and discouraging bad behaviors. If you are trying to discourage your pet from repeating a bad behavior (e.g., stealing food, tearing cushions, raiding garbage) or you are trying to keep them out of a particular area (e.g., the couch, bed, bathroom), then an environmental or pet-activated punishment maybe be the best way to go. Always ensure that before trying to stop whatever undesirable behavior your pet may have, try to present them with desirable alternative behavior. For example, if your pet is always jumping on the bed where they shouldn't be, try to provide them with a comfortable floor bed somewhere nearby.

Environmental punishments are things we can place in our house to discourage behavior from our pets such as motion detector sprays, upside-down carpet runners, bark-activated sprays, and aversive taste sprays, among other things. Remote punishments are punishments you can activate by remote from different parts of your house if your pet misbehaves, examples of these are remote sprays, remote alarms, and often simply spraying your pet while out of sight.

Negative punishment is based on reducing behavior by removing something pleasant from the environment around our pet. As an example, if you are playing with or giving affection to your pet and an undesired behavior starts to happen (e.g., scratching, biting, mounting), immediately look to put a halt to any playing or affection. This removal of something the pet enjoys is a negative punishment because you remove stimuli instead of adding it. Keep in mind, unless your dog can tell what negative action has caused these positive stimuli to be removed, the behavior they were showing may worsen as they get frustrated and confused for suddenly not receiving their positive stimuli.

Positive reinforcement happens if behavior is increased by something that is added (usually something pleasant); **negative reinforcement** happens if behavior is increased by removing something (usually something unwanted).

In positive reinforcement training, you want to reward your pet right away and every single time they perform the desired behavior until the behavior is consistently repeated. If the behavior is something you want to be trained into being repeated by a cue or command, a hand signal or word should be used before the reward is handed to your pet. Although rewards are used to positively reinforce behavior, a reward is not synonymous with positive reinforcement. A reward can be anything your dog enjoys, whether that be a walk, playing, getting petted, treats, toys, food, or chews. Just keep in mind, if there isn't a clear link between the behavior you want and the reward, then the reward will not have the desired effect on your pet or reinforce the correct behavior.

Negative reinforcement is not something you should confuse with punishment. Punishment always seeks to lessen the amount or severity of behavior, while reinforcement looks to promote good behavior. Negative reinforcement is rarely needed in dog training, but there are occasions where it may be used in tandem with other forms of training. Negative reinforcement plays into our pet's flight reflex, "If I run away, then I'll be safe." For example, if my anxious pet were to go to the dog park, they know that if they don't leave the car, they won't have to meet other dogs. So, taking this logic, if you want to train your dog to walk without pulling on the leash, you can place a head halter on them and put pressure on them until they comply. Once the dog complies, you can remove the pressure that will act as negative reinforcement. You reward them by removing discomfort. A big potential negative consequence of negative reinforcement can be that if your pet reacts badly to the pressure (e.g., aggression, anxiety), by removing the stimulus that is making them uncomfortable, the behavior that we were trying to avoid is reinforced. If you don't get your desired result, then you run the risk of reinforcing bad behavior.

Overlearning

Overlearning is less a technique on its own but more a reinforcement technique for other ways of training. If you have trained your dog to behave a certain way to certain stimuli, make sure to repeatedly evoke that positive response. This is frequently used for training dogs for professional purposes but can also be very effectively used for training fearful or anxious dogs. Overlearning helps reinforce three things:

1. It increases the chances that a learned behavior becomes a natural behavior.
2. It helps to remind our pet constantly of what to do in that scenario.
3. It reminds them of the reward system set in place for performing good behaviors.

Extinction

Extinction is classified as the ending of a behavior only after all reinforcement is removed. If your dog jumps up whenever you get home from work and you can't help but pet them, you are reinforcing this bad behavior. Instead, remove all reinforcement, don't pet them, and don't pay attention to your dog. This will eventually discourage your pet from performing that bad behavior to elicit a response from you. Keep in mind, if you slip up at any point during the process and pet him when you shouldn't, you will be prolonging the bad behavior. Also, be aware that the intensity of negative behaviors will increase before they are made extinct. Extinction may be something we want to practice in the case of this example, but it may also be something we want to avoid in the case of other forms of training. For many other forms of training, we want to continue encouraging good behavior with treats and rewards. By at any point stopping the rewards, we risk the extinction of the positive reactions we were getting. High-value rewards, occasional reinforcement, and plenty of practice all reduce the risk that good behaviors will go extinct.

Shaping

Shaping is the process of gradually shaping your dog's actions towards an end goal behavior. In shaping, you look to reward any behavior that resembles the desired behavior. For example, when teaching a dog to lay down, the dog sitting is a behavior worthy of a reward. By rewarding the sit, you increase the chances that this action will be repeated. This sitting behavior is only rewarded again when it more closely resembles an attempt to lay down. For every step closer to the desired end goal behavior, your pet should be rewarded. Once the final behavior has been reached, use shaping to increase the duration of the behavior, increase obedience, and make sure your pet stays relaxed.

Flooding

This is a training technique that is most commonly used to help treat fears of harmless stimuli that may affect your dog. The idea behind flooding is to force your pet to stay in the presence of the stimuli that frightens them until they realize that it is not going to harm them. This technique is rarely completely effective and has an equal chance to just increase the fear your pet feels. Using this method also has potentially negative implications on the long-term mental welfare of your pet. This practice also tends to increase the initial fear your pet feels from the stimulus and cannot be halted or stopped until all signs of fear and anxiety are gone; otherwise, you may see a severe resurgence of fear. If not done properly, flooding may therefore lead to more serious behavior problems.

In professional practice, flooding is often used in a similar way to desensitization. The fear-inducing stimulus is introduced on a small level to cause mild fear or anxiety and is kept there until the dog calms down and gets used to it. The dog is then presented with positive reinforcement in the shape of treats or attention. This process is repeated at higher levels until the dog is no longer afraid of the stimulus.

Chapter 7: Worst-Case Scenario

If the absolute worst-case scenario happens and your dog gets into an altercation with another dog, you need to be prepared. Dog fights tend to only last a few seconds, but those seconds could be the difference between a hurt ego and serious injury in your pet or others' pets. It can be a scary thing to witness, but with the right knowledge, you can easily break up a dog fight with no risk of injury to yourself or others.

How to Break up a Dog Fight

The process of breaking up a fight between two or more dogs is actually very straightforward. The thing most people struggle with is staying calm and level-headed amid all the panic. If you can stay calm and follow the procedure (outlined below), you will be able to easily break up any fight.

Dog Aggressions Management

Dogs Fighting

The Wheelbarrow

The wheelbarrow is the go-to method for most dog trainers. The only issue with this method is that you need two people to do it effectively. Two people grab the back legs of their dogs and pull them away from each other. This makes it impossible for the dogs to continue fighting and also protects the humans from getting bitten in the heat of the moment. Once you have separated the dogs, you and the other person will turn your dogs around, still holding their back legs, and walk them away from the other dog. This immediately stops the dogs from being able to fight, allows you to safely separate them, and keeps the people involved safe from being bitten.

If you are alone in breaking up the fight, try to follow these steps below:

Examine the Situation

If you are the only person present or able to break up the fight, the first step is always to figure out which dog is the aggressor. In every dog fight, there is always one animal that is more aggressive than the other. These fights usually start with one dog lashing out and the other defending itself; if you can figure out which dog *doesn't* want to be fighting, you can attempt to remove the other dog to stop the fight.

Break Any Grip the Dog May Have

When one dog latches on to another, it can be very risky to try and separate them before the grip is broken. Trying to pull away a dog that has a grip on another may just end up doing more harm to the bitten dog, and this could cause the biting dog to clamp down harder.

The best way to break the grip of a dog is to slide a "break stick" or a long flat stick into the mouth of the biting dog. Make sure the stick is horizontal when inserted and push it to the back of the biting dog's mouth, then twist it vertically. This will cause the biting dog to open its jaw and release its grip. Remember though, unless it is your dog(s), it's the owner's responsibility to get involved. If they are unable or incompetent, only then should you get involved.

Pull on the Dog's Collar

After breaking the dog's grip, it's important to immediately pull it away from the other dog. Remember to pull the collar directly back and low; if you raise the dog, exposing their chest and belly, you may just make them even more aggressive and panicked. Make sure to remain completely calm and assertive at this time. Don't shout too loudly as this may just cause even more confusion and anxiety in the dogs and people around. Use a stern and commanding voice when separating the dogs; this makes sure the dogs know you are a human in charge of the situation.

Move the Dogs Away From Each Other

The last stage of dealing with a dog fight is removing the dogs from each other's presence. It's important to make sure the two dogs are kept out of each other's sight and that both are kept on a leash. Dogs can move very fast and if one slips free, another fight can start in a matter of seconds.

What Should I Do If I Can't Break up a Fight?

There will be occasions where you can't break up a dog fight. You may not have the right tools present or the dogs may be too aggressive. If this is the case, it's best to stay out of the fight. People can end up with severe cuts, broken or crushed bones, or worse if they get involved in fights they are not equipped for. Think clearly and put your own safety first; never put your own well-being at risk to break up a dog fight. Getting involved in a fight that you are not equipped to stop can injure yourself and worsen things for the dogs involved, putting them at higher risk too.

Dog fights can be very serious, but the vast majority of the time they are over after a few seconds of struggling with minor injuries.

Make sure you know your own limitations and never try to overpower an animal that is too strong for you. Some larger breeds of dogs can be very dangerous when in fight or flight mode.

How Do I Prevent a Dog Fight?

The best way of breaking up a dog fight is to never let it happen in the first place. You may think that because Fido has never been in a fight before that he hasn't got it in him, but any dog is capable of being involved in a fight if all the right (or wrong) circumstances present themselves.

Does Your Dog Have a History of Aggression?

This may seem obvious to many of us looking in from the outside, but many people like to think that their aggressive dog is different: "Fido learned his lesson last time" or "It won't happen again. I smacked him real good after the last fight."

If your dog has *any* history of aggression, it's best to not take him out to public settings. For your safety, for your dog's safety, and for the safety of others, avoid the dog park or any other public place that will have many animals f. If you must take your pet out

106

for walks, do so with a muzzle and make sure you always have a good hold of the leash.

Read Their Body Language

As we've covered already, dog body language is a key factor in being able to predict what their mood and behavior is likely to be. A dog that is on the edge of lashing out or being aggressive has some telltale signs that may just help you avoid a dog fight. Look for the following signs of anxiety in your dog that may lead to aggression with other pets:

- Flattened ears
- Cowering
- Long and wide-mouthed yawn
- Licking lips
- Erect back hair
- Wide eyes (you can see the whites)
- Tucked or completely stiff tail

If you see any of these signs in your dog or another dog, make sure to remove that dog from the environment they are in and allow them to calm down. These signs may mean that the dog is one step away from feeling threatened and needing to defend itself.

Aggressive Snarl

What Should I Do After a Dog Fight?

If your dog or another dog gets involved in a fight, it's crucial that you know how to handle the situation after the fight has ended. The first few moments after a fight can determine if the situation is resolved or if another fight is on the brink of starting.

Remove the Dogs From the Environment

The first step is to remove the dogs from the area in which the fight took place. There may be other dogs around who are now all anxious and on edge. There may be people who are making a commotion, which can make the dogs more anxious, and of course, the dogs may try to fight again. So, we want to take both of the dogs involved, leash them both, and walk them away in opposite directions. If the dogs are injured, allow them to calm down and remove them by other means.

Calm Them Down

After removing the dogs from the situation they were in, they need to be calmed down. Make sure to talk to them in a soft and calm tone, use comforting words, and pet them if they allow you. This will help them calm down and recover from the trauma they just experienced. This can help avoid symptoms of post-traumatic stress and lessen your pet's anxiety towards other dogs in the future. Most dogs will recover from a minor fight in a matter of hours, but some dogs may take a bit longer.

Check for Injuries

Although usually minor, some dog fights can lead to serious injuries. With all the thrashing of teeth and claws, it is easy for damage to occur to the eyes, nose, and ears. Bites may leave nasty gashes and puncture wounds, which may need stitches to heal safely. Make sure to check each dog involved for cuts, bites, and abrasions. Be gentle and calm with your movements, thoroughly checking the dog's entire body with your eyes at first, then with your hands if the dog allows.

If there are any areas where your dog flinches or yelps, make sure to inspect those closely as there may be a wound there that is not initially clear to the eye. It is always wise to take your dog into a veterinary clinic after a fight and have them checked by a professional. A vet may be able to pick up on muscular or bone injuries that we will otherwise miss in our inspection.

Find Them a Safe Place

If your dog is in a good state, calm, and uninjured, it is best to now take them somewhere that they will feel safe. This is usually their home or a particular part of the house. Make sure to give them a quiet spot to recover, away from other pets and people. Give them plenty of praise, pets, treats, and rest. This may seem like you're rewarding bad behavior, but it is important that your dog recovers from this event and is in a healthy mental place if we hope to train them. If your dog is nervous of other pets after this event, try slowly desensitizing them to other dogs.

If Your Dog Needs Veterinary Attention

Dogs fighting can lead to serious injuries on rare occasions, and so you should always be prepared for the worst. If your dog gets seriously injured in a fight, you will need to rush them to a vet immediately. This means knowing where your nearest vet is and how to get there.

Make sure you are aware not only of the nearest vet in relation to your house but the nearest to your dog park or anywhere else that you frequently take your pet. If we know these details, whatever may happen, we can respond quickly and without hesitation. Make sure the vets in question are capable of performing emergency procedures; a lot of these vets will advertise specifically as *emergency animal hospitals*. These vets are typically open 24/7 and have all the facilities needed to treat whatever injury your dog may have. A normal neighborhood vet clinic may not be able to handle serious injuries.

If your dog is injured after the fight, it's best to try and carry them, if possible, to your car for transport to the nearest pet hospital. Keep in mind, carrying them may cause them pain depending on their injuries and this could cause them to bite or lash out. It is often recommended to place a towel or shirt over the dog's head to make them feel more secure and calm. If your pet is bleeding badly, make sure to use a piece of clothing or a towel to apply pressure to the area of bleeding. If you have to restrain your dog or apply pressure to wounds, kindly ask someone else to drive you and your dog to the pet hospital while you attend to your dog. Try to remain calm and composed; your pet will pick up on your calm demeanor. The worst thing that could happen right now is your injured animal feeling more anxious, panicking, and potentially hurting someone or itself more.

Most people don't know how to handle a dog fight or what comes after. Now that you do know, be sure to teach other pet owners. The more people who are aware and informed, the fewer dog fights there will be, and the fewer dogs may be injured or hurt. If you see someone incorrectly trying to break up a dog fight, make sure to intervene and take charge, not only for the good of the dogs but also for the safety of the people involved who may get injured. Using the tactics we have discussed here can save yourself, your dog, and others from serious injury.

Chapter 8: Pathways to Aggression

There are many pathways to aggression in dogs, and as you've seen, there are many different types of aggression. There are, however, a few pathways to aggression that could be considered the most common routes to aggression in normal household pets. These pathways to aggression revolve around either a lack of social skills or reinforcement of bad habits by the dog's owner. Of course, these are rarely intentional but nevertheless must be corrected to avoid possible issues with your pet in the future.

Lack of Socialization With Humans

It is recommended that puppies start learning how to socialize with people between the age of four weeks and four months. At this age, you should be introducing your pup to new people and letting it learn how to understand and read human behavior.

Dog Aggressions Management

Furthermore, your pup will start to pick up on the social cues needed for it to socialize with humans for the rest of its life.

This socialization early in a dog's life helps it to learn that new and different people don't mean "bad and scary." Having positive experiences with new people and places during those crucial first few weeks is incredibly important for creating a confident and sociable dog.

A pup that isn't socialized with people will be at constant risk of stress and anxiety when placed in social situations with humans or public places with lots of people. This could be a recipe for disaster, especially if the owner isn't aware of their pet's calming signals.

A dog that hasn't been socialized is very likely to suffer general fearfulness from the introduction of new people into its environment. This can be very troublesome if you decide to take your dog to the park or have people over. Your dog becomes stressed and likely to lash out because it is unable to tell if these people are friends or foes.

A dog that hasn't been socialized may also show an aversion to being handled by humans. This can be especially troublesome for vets and groomers who may need to handle your animal. An unsocialized animal can be potentially dangerous to a vet or groomer because it is far more likely to lash out and feel threatened by being handled by unfamiliar humans. Basic animal husbandry like nail clipping, teeth brushing, and cleaning may become nearly impossible for the owner too; a dog that is not made used to these actions from a young age will be very unlikely to sit still and tolerate them later in life.

A dog that lacks socialization may also struggle to adapt to new environments. Going for a drive in the car, a walk on the beach, a trip to a pet-friendly store, a hike, or even just a trip to the dog park may cause serious stress and anxiety in your dog. Even if there aren't other people around, just being out of their home environment may be enough to cause these dogs to suffer.

Tips for Socializing With Humans

If you have a dog that clearly is uncomfortable around new people and places, you will need to socialize them. Luckily, although it's best to do this with puppies, it is still possible to socialize older dogs.

Dog Aggressions Management

You just need the right approach and plenty of patience.

- **Daily Walks**: Walking your dog daily is the single best way of socializing them. Take it slow at first; only walking a block or two is enough to get your dog used to it. Once your dog is showing less anxiety, start to progressively walk further and into busier areas.

  When your dog has started to experience the world a bit, mundane things that may have scared them before like cars or strangers start to seem a bit less scary. Just make sure to keep your dog on a short leash and be aware of your pet's limits.

Dog Aggressions Management

Dog Walking

- **Introduce Variety**: Make sure to expose your pet to a wide variety of different people and places. Introduce your dog to men, women, and children, and all sorts of different places like buildings, streets, and parks. Your dog will grow afraid of strangers if they only hang out with one person every day. This makes it crucial to diversify your dog's outlook on the world.

  When introducing your dog to new people, make sure you stay calm and try not to force them. Don't make a big deal out of any negative behavior either. If people pet your dog, make sure it's in places where your dog can see their hands, like the chin or chest. Use treats for every positive encounter. And, once your pet is comfortable, feel free to hire a dog walker to get them used to different people walking them.

- **Dog Classes**: A great place to socialize your pet and get professional help may be dog training classes or socialization groups. Many training centers host regular group sessions specifically designed to help with pet socialization that offer a safe and controlled environment for you and your pet to learn and socialize with others.

Lack of Socialization With Animals

Similar to humans, we ideally want to socialize our dogs with other dogs when they are young. Puppies, in their first few months, learn how to effectively read and socialize with other dogs. Just as pups need to learn how to read the actions and body language of humans, they also need to learn how to read the body language of other dogs; otherwise, we may have to deal with the negative consequences of having a dog that doesn't know how to speak "dog."

A dog that is not introduced to other dogs at a young age will struggle to understand and pick up on the subtle social cues that dogs use to communicate. Not just that, a dog that hasn't spent time with others may not know how to communicate its own feelings in an appropriate way to other dogs. This, of course, could lead to a whole plethora of problems.

If your pet can't effectively communicate its thoughts and feelings to other dogs, you may just end up with a dog that accidentally causes aggression whenever they interact with others. Your dog may also just outright refuse to interact with other dogs out of fear. This fear can be compounded even further if other dogs approach yours and your animal is unable to communicate their discomfort. This can lead to your dog lashing out at others because it perceives them as a threat.

A lack of socialization with other dogs may also lead to your dog becoming sound sensitive in regards to barking. A dog that is unfamiliar with the sounds other dogs make can become anxious and confused by barking, even if it's only play-barking. This can become an issue if new animals move in next door or if your dog is taken to a dog park. Your pet may become frightened or even aggressive because of the sudden introduction of loud unfamiliar noises from other dogs.

And, of course, if your dog isn't familiar with doggy playstyles, even if they are able to communicate and approach other dogs without fear, they may just interpret a playful nip as a reason to fight. Play, among dogs, is an incredibly important part of social behavior. It helps build bonds and acts as a much-needed energy burner. It also helps your dog figure out the social dog hierarchy. If your dog is unfamiliar with playing with other dogs, it may be a very alien and overwhelming experience for them and could easily devolve into a fight or aggression.

Tips for Socializing With Other Dogs

If your dog has inexperience with other dogs and struggles in social scenarios, then it is important that you work towards socializing them. Luckily, just as with socializing dogs with humans, it is still possible to socialize your dog with other dogs even if they aren't a puppy or young dog anymore.

- **Have Plenty of Treats**: Dogs love treats. In fact, dogs will do almost anything for their favorite treat. Every time your dog has a successful interaction with another pet, give them a treat. Soon enough your dog will learn that this good behavior yields them good rewards. High-value treats will get the best reaction.
- **Set up Playdates**: A great way to get your dog used to other dogs in a controlled environment is by setting up playdates with friends or neighbors. Having one-on-one doggy play dates are a perfect way of easing your dog into a dog social environment. Just

make sure you are nearby to console your pet if they feel anxious, or encourage and reward them if they are doing well.

- **Visit the Dog Park or Pet Store**: Visiting the dog park or pet store shouldn't be your first action if you are trying to socialize your dog. These are intermediate steps but if your dog has been doing well in one-on-one scenarios, this might be the next step to take. The dog park is a great environment for your pet to meet other dogs and learn how to deal with groups.

This is an environment where your dog will also learn how to play in groups and learn a bit about social hierarchy. It's best to start out slow and consider getting an "I need space" vest for your dog so that others know not to overwhelm them. The pet store is a quieter space to take your dog as you are likely to come across a lot more one-on-one encounters here. By taking your dog to the pet store, they may also learn how to behave around other dogs in "human" environments.

Normal or Abnormal?

Dogs will always misbehave. It's natural for energetic, intelligent, inquisitive creatures. Many people are unable to tell the difference between normal behavior and abnormal behavior. There is a natural level of naughtiness that most dogs fall into, but anything more than that can be classified as abnormal or even pathologic. So, what is normal behavior and what is abnormal behavior for your dog?

First, you need to understand the innate behaviors associated with your dog's breed. Almost all breeds have been bred with a specific task in mind, so you may find that they have different innate traits. A Border collie, for example, may end up chasing cyclists because they are naturally bred to herd livestock and may try to herd the bicycle. A bloodhound may drag you in the direction of a new scent because they were bred to track and hunt. A Jack Russel might go crazy at a squirrel in your backyard tree because they were bred to chase down small mammals. Some dogs even repeat the survival instincts of their ancestors; for example, a husky may end up digging a hole in your yard for a nice warm place to sleep in.

Dog Aggressions Management

These actions are just your dog following their instincts, but these instincts can become problematic, especially if your dog ends up barking all day, digging up your garden, or chasing cyclists.

There are a few degrees of misbehavior that we can categorize our dog into. By understanding the degree of their misbehavior, we can figure out whether it's normal, abnormal, or pathologic.

1. **Normal Behavior for the Breed and Age of Dog**: Some behaviors may seem undesirable but are perfectly normal and will be grown out of. For example, puppies are always going to chew things when they are teething. Similarly, older dogs are always going to slow down and be less active than younger dogs. This isn't your dog being less sociable or depressed; this is old age.

2. **Behaviors That Are Within or Just Beyond Normal**: Most of the most common abnormal behaviors lay within this range. These are behaviors that are naturally normal but because of the time and place that our pet decides to do them, they become abnormal and problematic. For example, it's perfectly normal for our pet to mark their territory, but

marking their territory against the living room couch is unwanted abnormal behavior.

Understanding the reasons for this behavior (e.g., a new dog in the household) will help you to prevent it in the future and divert it elsewhere. Just make sure to keep your expectations realistic. Every now and then, you may have to clean up a little urine; that's part of being a dog owner.

3. **Behaviors That Are Abnormal or Pathologic in Nature:** Some behaviors are definitely abnormal or may even be considered pathologic. The difference between abnormal behavior and pathologic behavior can be slim at times but, for the most part, abnormal behavior is undesirable but not harmful (e.g., mounting, barking, urine-marking) and pathologic behavior can become harmful if not attended to (separation-anxiety, aggression, destructive impulses).

What may be abnormal to some people is acceptable with others. As long as the abnormal behavior isn't causing harm, inconvenience, or discomfort to you or your pet it is optional whether you want to correct it. All pathologic behavior, on the other hand, is potentially dangerous and inconvenient. If your animal shows any behavior that can be classed as pathologic, be sure to seek the help of a professional in correcting that behavior if your own training doesn't solve the problem.

The Way Owners Can Promote Unwanted Behavior

Dogs can be thought of just like children in many ways. If you don't raise them well, they are likely to act out. This is something many owners don't understand. It's easy to think that your dogs will just look after themselves, and they will, but that means they're going to find ways of entertaining themselves that you may not enjoy as much as them. Owners can promote aggression and unwanted behavior in several ways, but it all leads back to a lack of awareness and attention given to your pet.

No Supervision

Supervision is key when trying to make sure your pet is happy and well behaved. Not only do you want to supervise them so they don't get into trouble, but supervising your pet also means keeping an eye on them for triggers.

Always try to keep an eye on your pet and notice any new triggers they may develop; these triggers may be easily dealt with in the moment. If you can snub out negative behavior before it even starts, then you are avoiding hours of training work and lots of anxiety for your pet.

No Structure

Structure is important for your pet and yourself. If you have a schedule set up of feeding times, playtimes, walking times, and so on, it gives your pet something to look forward to each day.

By having a set time for your walks, your pet will happily wait knowing that their time to exercise and explore is coming. This will stop them from hopping the fence or making a mess of the garden. If you have a set time every day for feeding, that makes your pet far less likely to raid the garbage for something to eat, because they know for sure that food is coming.

No Exercise

A lack of exercise is one of the primary causes of frustration and anxiety in most breeds of dogs. It is incredibly important that you are able to take your dog on regular walks or set up regular playdates with other dogs. It may seem like a lot of work, which it is, but that's what you sign up for as a dog owner.

It becomes your responsibility to make sure your companion is healthy and fit. A dog with too much pent-up energy is a dog that becomes restless and stressed. That pent-up energy has to be released in one way or another, either happily through exercise or mischievously through unwanted behavior and potential aggression.

No Management

I've noticed that many new owners struggle with managing their dogs. What I mean by managing is taking charge, punishing them when they're wrong, and rewarding them when they're right. If you don't manage your dog properly, don't expect it to listen to you when you give commands or call its name.

Dog's respond to firm authoritative leadership; if you don't show this leadership, then your dog is going to lead themselves. Make sure that you always manage your pet in a respectful, firm, and caring way. One of the best ways to avoid any trouble in the future is having a dog that listens and does what it is told.

Accidentally Promoting Bad Behavior

With all the different techniques of training dogs and the different timings they involve, it may be easy to accidentally promote bad behavior. I often see cases of people struggling with their pets because they have accidentally been reinforcing the behavior they are trying to correct. For example, I often find people mess up the timing on desensitization training. Fido is scared of sirens; his owners play soft siren sounds, Fido gets scared, his owner turns off the sound and gives Fido a treat.

What did the owner do wrong? He turned off the sound before giving the treat. This teaches Fido that being scared makes the sound go away. You want to give Fido the treat before the sound goes off. This teaches him that the sound brings treats so it can't be *too* bad. Mistakes like this are incredibly common and can make an otherwise very mild cause of unwanted behavior into a serious case.

Additional Information on Dog Aggression Terms

While writing this book, I tried to keep things in as "plain English" as possible; there is a lot of jargon in the dog behavior field and I want this book to be understandable to anyone. The few jargon terms that I did use I tried to explain as well as possible, but just in case, I've included this section of additional information. Here you will find explanations of a few of the words we use that I feel need some more explanation. There are also a few words (e.g., fear, anxiety) that may mean more in the context of dog behavior than in just normal English. Lastly, I did include one or two words that weren't used in the book, but that relate directly to some of the content that you've covered.

Abnormal Behavior

These are activities that show dysfunctional actions or behavior. The terms behavior problem, unwanted behavior, and emotional disorder may also be commonly used. Abnormal behavior is typically behavioral complaints that are normal behaviors done in the wrong context or at unwanted places or times. (e.g., herding, resource guarding, garbage raiding, or urine marking).

Aggression

Aggression can be defined in two ways. In a narrow sense, it is attacking or fighting behavior. In a broader sense, it is antagonistic behavior. In the case of the latter, aggression can be appropriate (play fighting) or inappropriate (growling at humans), in context (the need to defend oneself) or out of context (learned behavior), or a challenge that will result in self-defense or resolution through fighting.

Anxiety

Anxiety in dogs is much like anxiety in humans. It is the worried anticipation of future danger and misfortune. This may be shown in both behavioral and physical signs (hypervigilance, tension, hyperactivity).

Conflict

Conflict, in the context of dogs, can be defined when a dog has motivations that compete or is motivated to try and perform more than one opposing behavior. An example of this is when a dog is motivated to play with other dogs but is scared to approach them. This can be caused by past unpleasant experiences (e.g., aggression). The resulting behavior can either be a displacement behavior or aggression (when fear becomes the dominant feeling).

Displacement Behavior

This type of action is typically a normal behavior that is done out of context or is "displaced" because the dog is not able, either physically or mentally, to perform another activity or occupy itself. This is different from redirected behavior because the behavior is not directed towards a specific target.

When displacement behavior happens, the behavior is almost always out of the context of the situation (e.g., ground sniffing, urination, snapping at the air). These behaviors may happen from conflict, frustration, or as a vacuum activity.

Dominance

Dominance is frequently wrongly applied or misunderstood. The ethological (natural animal behavior) concept of dominance describes it as control over a resource that is limited and the ability for a stronger or higher-ranking animal to control whether a lower-ranking one has access to that resource. The rank of an animal is defined as its ability to control limited resources, control others' access to resources, and control access to mating.

Dominance is not the same as hierarchical rank. Ranks are not based on access to resources and are rather based on the character of an animal and ability to respond appropriately to social and environmental cues. Confident and assertive postures and signals from one dog will lead to a more "dominant" rank if the second dog displays subordinate behavior in return. However, dominant and subordinate does not describe these two dogs unless the pattern holds true over both resources and interactions. Dominance is control or resources. Rank is a confident and assertive character.

Fear

Fear is the feeling of worry that is associated with the presence of an object, social situation, or individual. Fear is normal behavior and an adaptive response (self-preservation). To figure out whether the fearful response of a dog is abnormal or unwanted has to be decided by the context of the situation. For example, fire is a common enough part of life, but avoiding fire is an instinctual adaptive response. If a pet is fearful of stimuli that are harmless, like certain sounds or surfaces, that fear is irrational and, if constant, would become abnormal behavior.

Frustration

A state of frustration arises when an animal feels motivated to engage in behaviors that it is not able to fulfill because of a physical or psychological barrier in its environment. When a pet is frustrated, such as your dog not being able to chase a squirrel in the garden because of a door keeping him inside, the resulting frustration might become redirected behavior (e.g., aggression towards another pet or person), displacement behavior (e.g., pacing, scratching), or anxiety (e.g., howling, barking).

Redirected Behavior

Redirected behaviors are actions that are directed away from the primary target and toward another nearby inappropriate target. When a dog is in a position where it may be emotionally aroused and it is unable to reach the target of its arousal, the frustration may get redirected to an alternative target if the animal is bothered or interrupted. For example, if your dog desperately wants to go outside to bark at the postman, and your other pet walks by, your emotionally aroused dog may just lash out its frustration on the other dog.

Vacuum Activity

A vacuum activity is when your dog is highly motivated to act out an instinctual behavior but there is no possible way for them to do so at that moment. The anxiety from that may cause a vacuum activity to then be acted out (e.g., licking, tail chasing). Activities like this have no useful purpose and just serve as a way of keeping your dog occupied in moments of mild anxiety.

Busting Some Myths

There are a few interesting myths and misconceptions that surround dogs and their relationship to our world. Some of the most common myths about dogs may majorly impact the way we interact with them and, therefore, impact our relationships with them.

All of these common misconceptions directly relate to the subject of this book and influence the way that dogs are often treated. I hope that by addressing these myths and laying them to rest, you can build a better understanding of your companion.

Dogs Are Colorblind

It's tough to trace back the origin of this myth, and we can never confirm it for sure because none of us can see what a dog sees. But, structurally, the retina of a dog contains two of the three photoreceptor types needed to see color. Experiments have shown that they can see a multitude of colors, including different shades and depths of blue, yellow, and grey.

Dog Aggressions Management

The range of color they see is definitely less than ours, but they are capable of distinguishing items based on their color. Bright colors have been shown to actually attract the attention of dogs; this means that when training your pets, it may be beneficial to use brightly colored toys and treats to keep your dog's attention.

Shepherd With Flowers

A Wagging Tail Means a Friendly Dog

You've already seen mention of tail wagging as a calming signal, which already partially puts this misconception to rest. No, a wagging tail does not always mean a friendly dog. A low wagging tail can mean a dog that is anxious and trying to show submission. A slow and high wagging tail can mean a dog that is focused on prey. An upright and stiff tail can mean a dog that is trying to show confidence and assertiveness. An aggressive dog may even wag its tail fast while barking at a perceived threat. Always study a dog's body language closely before approaching, or better yet, never approach a dog you don't know without talking to its owner first.

Dogs Eat Grass When They Feel Unwell

It is true that dogs eat grass to help deal with nausea. However, dogs also eat grass out of boredom and displacement behaviors. Some dogs just like eating grass because it's something that they might find fun to do. For the vast majority, this is not an issue unless the grass has been treated with a chemical treatment. So, as long as your dog only eats small amounts of grass, and it doesn't make them ill doing so, there is no reason for you to worry about this behavior. Grass eating may also be a displacement behavior that your dog acts out when anxious or frustrated.

One Dog Year Equals Seven Human Years

This myth is wildly false; in fact, the first year of a dog's life can be equal to around 12 to 14 human years. A dog's age is mainly dependent on a few primary factors such as breed, size, and genetics. The average small dog will live between 15 and 18 human years if it has had a healthy life. The average large or giant breed of dog may live up to around 10 human years of age. Most medium breeds are stuck somewhere in the middle, around 11 to 13 human years of age.

Knowing the rate at which dogs age is important for those who want to train their pets at the ideal age. While you may think a three-year-old dog is still nearly a puppy, that dog is actually equivalent to someone in their 30s. The first year of a dog's life is when they do the most ageing and maturing, and therefore, it is the most important time to imprint training and lessons on your dog.

You Can't Teach an Old Dog New Tricks

This one is definitely false. Older dogs can definitely learn new tricks, they just tend to be less active or more stubborn. Like with humans, as dogs age, they become less interested in learning new actions and are less likely to respond to training. Keep in mind, some older dogs also have worse hearing and joint issues that can make training a bit more challenging for them. With time and patience, an older dog can easily learn a new trick that any younger dog can learn. This is important to understand for owners looking to adopt older pets. Regardless of the age of the dog, learned behaviors can be changed through training and conditioning.

Conclusion

If you were still wondering about what happened to Spot, well, he recovered from his time at the trainers pretty quickly once I got him home and gave him some of his favorite treats. He may have forgotten about the whole experience in just a few days, but it stuck with me. In the months following that day, I joined a few local dog training clubs, took courses and classes in training, and eventually after a lot more work, I earned my qualifications in dog behavior and training. Spot got the attention and help he deserved and he went on to be the perfect family dog. He especially loves children and their non-stop energy, which matches his. This type of happy ending is what I hope for anyone that decides to read this book. Every dog deserves to live a happy life without fear and anxiety. And every pet owner deserves to have a happy and normal dog they can call their best friend.

With the knowledge you have gained from reading this book, I hope you are able to help yourself and your pet overcome the challenges you faced together. I hope that I was able to save one more potentially aggressive dog from a sad end, and one more owner from having to go through that loss.

Good luck. I wish the best for you and your pet, and if anyone you know needs help with an aggressive dog, you too will now have the knowledge to save that animal!

Bluesource And Friends

This book is brought to you by Bluesource And Friends, a happy book publishing company.

Our motto is **"Happiness Within Pages"**

We promise to deliver amazing value to readers with our books.

We also appreciate honest book reviews from our readers.

Connect with us on our Facebook page www.facebook.com/bluesourceandfriends and stay tuned to our latest book promotions and free giveaways.

References

Casey, R. A., Loftus, B., Bolster, C., Richards, G. J., & Blackwell, E. J. (2014). Human directed aggression in domestic dogs (Canis familiaris): Occurrence in different contexts and risk factors. *Applied Animal Behaviour Science*, 152(), 52–63. https://doi.org/10.1016/j.applanim.2013.12.003

CCSPCA. (2017, January 18). *How to Break Up a Dog Fight the Right Way*. Central California SPCA, Fresno, CA. https://www.ccspca.com/blog-spca/education/how-to-break-up-a-dog-fight/

Coren, S. (2017, February 22). *Are There Behavior Changes When Dogs Are Spayed or Neutered? Psychology Today*. https://www.psychologytoday.com/za/blog/canine-corner/201702/are-there-behavior-changes-when-dogs-are-spayed-or-neutered

Duffy, D., & Serpell, J. (2006). *Session I: Non-reproductive Effects of Spaying and Neutering PRESENTATION SUMMARY & POWERPOINT Non-reproductive Effects of Spaying and Neutering on Behavior in Dogs* [PDF]. Naia Online. https://www.naiaonline.org/uploads/WhitePapers/Ea rlySNAndBehaviorDuffySerpell.pdf

Holloway, A. (2017, December 6). *Dog behaviour explained | Normal & abnormal behaviours | Clent Hills Vets*. Clent Hills Vets. https://www.clenthillsvets.co.uk/dog-

behaviour-explained-normal-abnormal-dog-
behaviours/

Horwitz, D., & Landsberg, G. (n.d.). *Dog Behavior Problems - Aggression - Family Members - Treatment.* Vca_corporate. https://vcahospitals.com/know-your-pet/dog-behavior-problems---aggression---family-members---treatment

James Wellbeloved. (2017, August). D*og Body Language: Understanding My Dog.* https://www.wellbeloved.com/taking-care-of-my-dog/how-to-understand-my-dog/

Landsberg, G. (2014, May). *Glossary of Behavioral Terms - Behavior.* Veterinary Manual. https://www.msdvetmanual.com/behavior/behavioral-medicine-introduction/glossary-of-behavioral-terms

Lexico. (n.d.). Idiopathic. In *Lexico.com dictionary.* Retrieved February 18, 2021, from https://www.lexico.com/definition/idiopathic

Martin, K., & Buzhardt, L. (2009). *Aggression in Dogs.* Vca_corporate. https://vcahospitals.com/know-your-pet/fear-vs-aggression

McGreevy, P. D., Thomson, P. C., Pride, C., Fawcett, A., Grassi, T., & Jones, B. (2005). Prevalence of obesity in dogs examined by Australian veterinary practices and the risk factors involved. *Veterinary Record,* 156(22), 695–702. https://doi.org/10.1136/vr.156.22.695

Dog Aggressions Management

Nutrena. (n.d.). *Dog Myths and Misconceptions* | *Nutrena*.https://www.nutrenaworld.com/blog/dog-myths-and-misconceptions

PetMD. (2016, August 29). *7 Dangers of Not Socializing Your Dog*. https://www.petmd.com/dog/slideshows/7-dangers-not-socializing-your-dog

Sanborn, L. J., & Katz, L. S. (2007). *Long-Term Health Risks and Benefits Associated with Spay / Neuter in Dogs* [PDF]. Naia Online. http://www.naiaonline.org/pdfs/LongTermHealthEffectsOfSpayNeuterInDogs.pdf

Todd, Z. (2018, July 11). *What is Desensitization and Counter-Conditioning in Dog Training?* Companion Animal Psychology. https://www.companionanimalpsychology.com/2018/07/what-is-desensitization-and-counter.html

Vuckovic, A. (2017, November 30). *Aggression in Dogs: Signs, Causes, Types, And Solutions*. Petcube. https://petcube.com/blog/dog-aggression/

Image References

Dogs Playing. (2020, December 22). Retrieved from https://unsplash.com/photos/s79swOM_C6E/

Sad Black Lab. (2016, January 11). Retrieved from https://unsplash.com/photos/if5drRE4OM0/

Teeth Bared. (2018, July 31). Retrieved from https://unsplash.com/photos/bbiDkAEmC9s

Protective Mother. (2020, June 20). Retrieved from https://unsplash.com/photos/NOiWWYPIgAE

Under the Gate. (2016, April 11). Retrieved from https://unsplash.com/photos/UcBbUBvfrIw/

Golden Snarl. (2014, April 21). Retrieved from https://pixabay.com/photos/dog-angry-dog-aggressive-snappy-329280/

Post-Op Cone. (2021, February 6). Retrieved from https://pixabay.com/photos/dog-puppy-pet-cone-pet-animal-5987013/

Obese Dog. (2019, August 8). Retrieved from https://pixabay.com/photos/thick-dog-lie-watch-fat-large-4392363/

Nervous Yawn. (2017, August 9). Retrieved from https://pixabay.com/photos/dog-pet-golden-retriever-yawn-2619108/

Dog Aggressions Management

Panting Dog. (2019, April 18). Retrieved from https://pixabay.com/photos/dog-dog-look-tongue-pant-hybrid-4135347/

Hiding Dog. (2018, December 7). Retrieved from https://pixabay.com/photos/dog-animals-nursery-eyes-view-3855224/

Wagging Tail. (2019, August 22). Retrieved from https://pixabay.com/photos/dog-happy-tail-wagging-young-4421494/

Doggy Treats. (2014, May 21). Retrieved from https://pixabay.com/photos/dog-bones-puppy-pet-dog-food-food-350093/

Gentle Touch. (2016, November 28). Retrieved from https://pixabay.com/photos/dog-labrador-pet-canine-companion-1861839/

Dogs Fighting. (2016, March 2). Retrieved from https://pixabay.com/photos/dogs-mammals-order-of-precedence-1231010/

Aggressive Snarl. (2017, June 18). Retrieved from https://pixabay.com/photos/dog-angry-teeth-danger-breed-2414477/

Dog Walking. (2018, March 15). Retrieved from https://pixabay.com/photos/dog-canine-mammal-animal-white-dog-3226922/

Dog Training (2015, March 16). Retrieved from https://pixabay.com/photos/dachshund-dog-school-dog-training-672780/

Dog Aggressions Management

Shepherd With Flowers (2016, November 23). Retrieved from https://pixabay.com/photos/flowers-dog-shepherd-puppy-spring-1845074/

Graying Old Dog (2017, September 10). Retrieved from https://pixabay.com/photos/eurasians-medium-spitz-like-dog-2735337/

Printed in Great Britain
by Amazon